Hotels & Restaurants

1830 to the present day

Priscilla Boniface

GENERAL EDITOR
Peter Fowler

ROYAL COMMISSION ON HISTORICAL MONUMENTS ENGLAND

LONDON HER MAJESTY'S STATIONERY OFFICE

ISBN 0 11 700993 8

HER MAJESTY'S STATIONERY OFFICE

Government Bookshops

49 High Holborn, London, WC1V 6HB
13a Castle Street, Edinburgh EH2 3AR
41 The Hayes, Cardiff CF1 1JW
Brazennose Street, Manchester M60 8AS
Southey House, Wine Street, Bristol BS1 2BQ
258 Broad Street, Birmingham B1 2HE
80 Chichester Street, Belfast BT1 4JY

*Government publications are also available
through booksellers*

ACKNOWLEDGEMENTS

The Commission is grateful for permission to reproduce photographs
in the National Monuments Record of which the copyright is held
by:
Architectural Press
Batsford
B.W.S. Publishing (*Architect and Building News*)
Guildhall Library
Howarth-Loomes Collection
Mewès and Davis
Christopher Wood Gallery
The author thanks numerous colleagues on the Commission staff,
especially Miss J. Carden, Mr R. Flanders, Mrs D. Kendall and staff
in the Order Section and Mr R. Parsons and staff in the Photographic
Section.
Mr G. Warren, HMSO, has taken a most helpful personal interest
in applying his professional skills in design.

front cover Grand Hotel Scarborough. N. Yorkshire. Cuthbert Broderick, 1867.
N.M.R. 1980. *inside front cover* The Court, Adelphi Hotel, Liverpool,
Merseyside. Frank Atkinson, 1911–14. Bedford Lemere, 1914. *inside back
cover* The Restaurant, Claridges', London. Oswald Milne, 1930. Herbert
Felton, *c* 1930.

Printed in England for Her Majesty's Stationery Office by
Balding + Mansell, Wisbech.
Dd 699040 C 110

EDITOR'S FOREWORD

All the photographs in this book are held in the National Monuments Record (NMR), a national archive which is part of the Royal Commission on Historical Monuments (England). The NMR originated in 1941 as the National Buildings Record which, at a time when so much was being destroyed, took upon itself the task of photographing as many historic buildings as possible before it was too late. The Record continued its work after the War and was transferred to the Royal Commission in 1963. As the NMR, it now covers both architectural and archaeological subjects and contains well over a million photographs, together with maps, plans and other documents, relating to England's man-made heritage. The NMR is a public archive, open from 10.00 – 17.30 hours on weekdays; prints can be supplied to order on payment of the appropriate fee.

This book is the first of a series intended to illustrate the wealth of photographic material publicly available in the NMR. Many of the photographs are valuable in their own right, either because of their age or because of the photographer who took them or because they are the only records we now possess of buildings, and even whole environments, which have disappeared. Unlike other Commission publications, these are primarily picture-books, drawing entirely on what happens to be in the NMR. There is no attempt to treat each subject comprehensively nor to accompany it with a deeply researched text, but the text and captions are intended to give meaning to the photographs by indicating the context within which they can be viewed. It would be pleasing if they suggested lines of enquiry to others to follow up.

The early titles in the series will show where the strengths of the archive lie. Equally, of course, the collection is weak in some respects, and I hope that many of those who buy this volume may be reminded of old, and perhaps disregarded, photographs of buildings in their possession. We would be glad to be told of the whereabouts of such photographs as potential contributions to a national record of our architectural heritage.

Hotels and restaurants, unlike castles and cathedrals, may not be immediately obvious parts of that heritage. Yet, everyday things though they may be, as types of building they have a history and, in reflecting social change, they also become historical evidence. Through photographers with the foresight to record what was for them contemporary, we are able to illustrate here aspects of recent history from its mundane, sometimes already destroyed, 'monuments'.

Royal Commission on Historical
Monuments (England)
Fortress House,
23 Savile Row,
London W1X 1AB

Peter Fowler
Secretary,
Royal Commission on
Historical Monuments (England),
General Editor,
NMR Photographic Archives

SELECT BIBLIOGRAPHY

Marcus Binney and D. Pearce (eds.) *Railway Architecture*. Orbis Publishing 1979
(Chapter on Railway Hotels by Christopher Monkhouse).
Harold P. Clunn, *London Rebuilt 1897–1927*. John Murray 1927.
Harold P. Clunn, *The Face of London*. Simpkin Marshall 1932.
Harold P. Clunn, *The Face of the Home Counties*. Simpkin Marshall 1936.
Nicholas Cooper, *The Opulent Eye*. Architectural Press 1976.
H. J. Dyos and Michael Wolfe (eds). *The Victorian City*. Routledge & Kegan Paul 1973.
Greater London Council, *Liverpool Street Station*. Academy Editions 1978.
C. Matthew and D. Martin, *A Different World*. Paddington Press 1976.
Hugh Montgomery-Massingberd and David Watkin, *The London Ritz*. Aurum 1980.
Nathaniel Newnham-Davis, *Dinners and Dining*. Grant Richards 1899.
Nathaniel Newnham-Davis, *The Gourmet's Guide to London*. Brentanos 1914.
Donald J. Olsen, *The Growth of Victorian London*. Batsford 1976.
Derek Taylor and David Bush, *The Golden Age of British Hotels*. Northwood 1974.

MORLEY'S HOTEL.

Hotels & Restaurants

INTRODUCTION

Two factors influenced the establishment of large hotels and restaurants in England. The first was changing methods of travel; the second was a small number of companies and men who created, anticipated or responded to changes in public taste.

Before the 19th century, travel was by coach and horse or on foot and a large number of coaching inns, fairly small distances apart, catered for short-stay travellers. Visitors wishing to stay longer, perhaps for the season at a fashionable spa or resort, would often take lodgings or stay in a boarding house *en famille*. In London, until the mid-19th century, small family hotels like Morley's and Mivarts (later Claridge's) were the norm.

Before 1850, public dining-rooms were dingy and uninviting. There were the Clubs and a few luncheon bars in the City, but the majority of people 'eating out' would be served plain English food in the dining-rooms of inns or taverns.

The large railway companies, with the exception of the South Western, were not slow to realize the advantages of providing hotels and refreshment at major railway stations and termini. The stations were often not in the centres of towns nor near existing inns, so the provision of accommodation was a benefit to travellers, particularly as they sometimes needed a bed for the night as a result of their train being late. Most of the London termini had hotels nearby but the hotel at Euston was the first erected by a railway company, the London and Birmingham in 1839. The Great Western Hotel at Paddington (P. C. Hardwick in 1852) was the second. The latter was both large and luxurious and set a style for other railways to follow or improve upon.

Resorts flourished if they were lucky enough to be near a railway. In 1863 two Gothic-style hotels opened in Devon, The Ilfracombe Hotel, Ilfracombe (C. W. Hornes), and the Duke of Cornwall Hotel, Plymouth (C. Foster Hayward). Scarborough was an early resort which developed because of the discovery of a chalybeate and saline mineral spring, and it benefitted from the arrival of the railway. The Grand Hotel, Scarborough, was built in 1867. The northern industrial cities often acquired several railway hotels as a result of being main stopping points of rival railway companies each with stations, usually with hotels nearby, e.g. Liverpool, Bradford, Leeds.

Before 1860 London was ill-equipped with hotel accommodation, unlike North American and European cities. The

Pl. 19

Pl. 22

Westminster Palace Hotel was built in 1860, the first grand hotel not near one of the London railway termini and not erected by a railway company. Two years later the Langham Hotel (Giles and Murray) opened in Portland Place, a long way from the stations and Belgravia. It was, however, near embassies and had an Ambassador's Audience Room. The hotel advertised itself as being 95 feet above the Thames high-water mark, presumably because this was regarded as being healthy. The Midland Grand Hotel opened at St Pancras in 1873, but, with few exceptions such as railway hotels, Albert Smith's all embracing criticisms in *The English Hotel Nuisance* (1855) would have applied to accommodation in London (and the provinces) until 1880. Then Charles Dickens' *Dictionary of London* found hotels improved though still inadequate.

Frederick Gordon, innovative son of a decorator of newly emerging middle-class dining-rooms, changed the hotel and restaurant scene, beginning in the 1870s and remaining influential for fifty years. He was a solicitor, brother-in-law of Horatio Davies owner of Pimms, and had opened a restaurant called Crosby Hall in the City. He then opened the Holborn Restaurant, correctly gauging the requirements of businessmen by providing a number of banqueting rooms in addition to the usual dining-room, all in a large complex. In 1881, having established good City connections, he opened a large, luxurious hotel called the Grand in newly constructed Northumberland Avenue. Perhaps, for the first time, this catered for the middle classes and, unusually, allowed non-residents to eat *table d'hôte* dinner in the hotel. The formula worked. Gordon opened the First Avenue Hotel in High Holborn and, in 1885, the Metropole in

Northumberland Avenue. He later acquired from Jabez Balfour a third hotel, the Victoria, in Northumberland Avenue, opening it in 1887. Jabez Balfour, M.P., the 'genius who jumped at Park Lane and landed on Broadmoor', had formed the Liberator Building Co., and, having also built the Hyde Park Hotel (then flats named Hyde Park Court), he ran out of funds for the Hotel Cecil, completed after his imprisonment. Frederick Gordon then bought the Victoria for a reasonable price.

The clientele of the three Gordon hotels were described at the time as: 'Grand-old country families or heads of great firms in the north'; Victoria – 'Americans and Australians . . . well-dressed polite folk'; Metropole – 'those who have acquired large sums in business'.

A company named Spiers and Pond, formed by two Englishmen who had catered with considerable success in Australia, was improving restaurant facilities. They opened the Holborn Viaduct Hotel next to the station in 1874 and also provided the catering in the refreshment rooms at this and other stations. The Criterion Restaurant, a huge complex of rooms opened in 1873, and the Gaiety Theatre and Restaurant were also theirs. Throughout the 1880s and 1890s it was usual for restaurants to include musical entertainment and to have decorated rooms in different styles, e.g. Café Monico, Romano's, Trocadero. Both hotels and restaurants in the 1880s were often more ornate than stylish; quality and comfort were to some extent still missing.

Richard D'Oyly Carte, impresario and owner of the new Savoy Theatre, was impressed by American hotels and determined to provide the same type of service in his new Savoy Hotel. Like so many hoteliers since, he built the hotel to

Pl. 63 Central Railway's Marylebone Station opened, much later than the other London terminus hotels. The Great Central Railway had run short of money so the hotel was financed by Sir Blundell Maple's Frederick Hotels, named after Frederick Gordon, who had been asked to sit on the board. A close relationship had existed between Maple and Frederick Gordon since Maple and Co., founded by John Maple, John Blundell Maple's father, had contracts to furnish a number of hotels including those of Frederick Gordon. It was easier and financially beneficial for an hotel to contract to one firm for curtains, carpets and furniture rather than deal with several suppliers. Sometimes, however, hotels just hired 50, 51, 73, 74, 6, 7, 8, 9, 10, 11 furniture. Another firm, Waring and Gillow, was responsible for the furnishings of a number of hotels e.g. Hotel Cecil, Ritz, Liverpool Adelphi.

By 1900, the hotel boom in London had peaked. D'Oyly Carte had acquired Claridge's in 1893 and the Berkeley in 1901. He brought the chef from Paillards, a well known restaurant in Paris, to Pl. 39 Claridge's. The restaurant at the Berkeley also had a high reputation and was 72, 73 immensely fashionable. The Ritz (Mewès and Davis) opened in 1906 and the Piccadilly Hotel (Norman Shaw) in 1908. Against the prevailing climate of the pre-war period, J. Lyons were enormously successful financially; they produced a dividend of 42½ per cent for four years Pl. 83 in a row. Corner Houses mushroomed, and Lyons built the first stage of the Pl. 75 Strand Palace Hotel in 1907.

Although railway hotels did not decline, the bicycle and then the motor car made it possible for hotels to prosper in more remote localities. A former Governor-General of Canada, the 4th Earl Grey, devised a scheme whereby each county should set up a trust to run country hotels. He intended to steer a middle road between prohibition and the dictates of brewers. Hertfordshire was the most successful county in the venture and part of the emblem of Hertfordshire was adopted for the symbol of the new group, called the Public House Trust. After the First World War the name was changed to Trust Houses.

In 1910 restaurants joined with hotels in a renamed Association of Hotels and Restaurants. A number of hotels were requisitioned during the First World War which helped to solve the problem of a glut of hotels no longer making much, if any, profit. Sir Francis Towle, son of Sir William, then Chairman of Gordon Hotels, commented in 1928 that nowadays a great hotel resembled a battleship: it tended to become obsolete after twenty years of existence. He was speaking of the decision to sell the Grand, Northumberland Avenue. His brother, Arthur, was in charge of all London, Midland and Scottish Railway Hotels after the 1914–18 war.

In the inter-war period Trust Houses had acquired huge numbers of coaching inns, which suddenly found themselves back in demand due in large part to Mr Ford of Detroit. A number of hotels in London were revamped to cater for the tastes of 'Bright Young Things'. The Dorchester was built in 1930 but Gordon Pl. 89 Hotels, somewhat thankfully one suspects, sold it to McAlpines, the builders of the hotel, in 1936. J. Lyons opened the Cumberland Hotel and the associated Maison Lyons, which was decorated by Oliver Bernard. The Canadian Pacific Railway had acquired premises on the corner of Berkeley Square and Bruton Street for an hotel but this was not built. As rather a last gasp, in 1933, the London, Midland and Scottish Co. built a remarkable hotel at

Morecambe designed by Oliver Hill and the company rebuilt the Queen's Hotel, Leeds. A project for an addition to the Midland, Manchester, did not go ahead.

Pl. 91, 92

Restaurants fared somewhat better. Another Prince of Wales, later Edward VIII, dined and danced in public. He went regularly to the Embassy Club on Thursdays and the smart set went too. Music was still considered a complement to dinner and the Big Bands played on, often for dancing. Fischers in Bond Street was a stylishly designed restaurant with dance floor and, of course, a cocktail bar. There were a number of elegant restaurants in the St James's area, a fashionable place to live for men about town of the type described by P. G. Wodehouse. Quaglino's is one such restaurant which survives. Leicester Square was revitalized by the arrival of the movies. There were several large cinemas in the Square and fast-food restaurants in the area flourished. Often, as once they had been built in conjunction with theatres, restaurants were now included in cinema buildings.

Most fashionable seaside resorts had been going into a decline since the turn of the century. Members of the aristocracy had developed a taste for wintering in the south of France and during the 'twenties and 'thirties often spent summer holidays abroad too, in particular at French resorts like Biarritz. Cruises were taken on private yachts in the Mediterranean and Atlantic crossings on glamorous ships were also popular. For the first time travel could be by aeroplane. English resorts were left to cater for the masses who were unable to afford foreign travel.

The immediate post-Second World War period was one of considerable hardship. Somehow the rich leisured few never re-emerged to frequent smart restaurants and night-clubs. It was no longer considered enough to be 'amusing'. Few gentlemen did not work. Dinner parties were held in private houses, the food often showing the influence of Elizabeth David.

The availability of air travel to all and the foreign package holiday transformed the restaurant and hotel scene in the 1960s. There was a two-way traffic: the English sampled foreign cuisine in its home setting and consequently expected more from food in England. Bistros and Chinese restaurants proliferated. Foreign tourists, with Americans still in the forefront, invaded England and more particularly London, and skyscraper hotels were built anywhere between Heathrow and the West End.

Sir Richard Seifert, writing in the *Architect and Building News* in November 1970 on the hotels of the future, said that the biggest influence was airline tourism. Hotels would reduce the number of public rooms, and conference rather than banqueting facilities would be provided. Three hundred to a thousand rooms were likely, possibly even two thousand or more. Large foyers would be needed to process the increased number of guests. He said the typical hotel guest is a short-term visitor, probably travelling as one of a party.

Transport, then, continues to be the major influence on hotel architecture and design. Sixty-seven years ago Sir William Towle wrote in the Jubilee issue of *Railway News*:

'the nation owes a great debt of gratitude to the railway companies for the provision of many good hotels which would certainly never have been built by other capital.'

1 COCK TAVERN, FLEET STREET, LONDON.
Originally The Cock Alehouse, opened in the early 16th century. Pepys
records 'April 23, 1668 – Thence by water to the Temple, and there to the
Cock Alehouse, and drank, and eat a lobster, and sang, and mightily merry.
So almost night, I carried Mrs Pierce home . . .' The tavern was famous for its
chops and steaks and latterly only gentleman diners were admitted. The
building was demolished in 1886 but the tavern transferred to another site in
Fleet Street, where several of the old fittings were incorporated.

Until well into the 19th century it was the norm to dine at inns, of which
the Cock Tavern is an example, or chop-houses. Light refreshment could be
taken at coffee houses.

The illustration of the dining-room of the Cock Tavern, painted by
Crowther, an early recorder of threatened buildings, was probably executed
in the 1880s prior to demolition. Copyright Guildhall Library.

2 BEDFORD HOTEL, BRIGHTON, EAST SUSSEX.
The Bedford, designed by Thomas Cooper, was an early example of a grandiose type of hotel. It was opened in 1829.

The attractions of Brighton were greatly enhanced by the Prince Regent's attachment to the place. Sidney Newbery, 1945.

3 SIMPSON'S, Nos. 101–103 STRAND LONDON.
Simpson's was opened in 1848. It featured a cigar divan on the second floor, which was a café for gentlemen where they could read English and foreign newspapers, play chess for a fee and, on additional payment, receive a cigar and a cup of coffee. A ladies' room was upstairs and, contrary to the current norm, an *à la carte* dinner was served. Simpson's was rebuilt in 1903–4 because of its incorporation in the Savoy Hotel extension. It continues to serve traditional English fare.

The photograph shows the original Simpson's building. Copyright B. T. Batsford, *c* 1900.

ADELPHI HOTEL, LIVERPOOL, MERSEYSIDE.

The first Adelphi Hotel probably owed its success in part to the emergence of Liverpool as the main port for shipping on the North American route. Charles Dickens stayed at the hotel on his way to America in 1842 and was very fond of the cuisine.

Subsequently, a second hotel was built on the site *c* 1861 to the design of W. and A. Moseley, despite its proximity to the North Western Hotel at Lime Street Station. It was acquired by the London Midland Co. in 1890 for £105 000.

A final Adelphi Hotel was built between 1911–14, designed by Frank Atkinson, one of the architects of Selfridges. He intended his building to enclose an inner courtyard but the back was not built.

4 The photograph from a stereoscopic card shows the first Adelphi Hotel, Liverpool, in the 1850s. Copyright Howarth-Loomes Collection

5 The second Adelphi Hotel. Photographs taken for the London Midland and Scottish Co., *c* 1896.

6 The last Adelphi Hotel, Liverpool. Bedford Lemere, 1914.

7 The Fountain Court. Bedford Lemere, 1912.

8 Drawing Room with furnishings by Waring and Gillow. Bedford Lemere, 1914.

9 The Hypostyle Hall. Bedford Lemere, 1912.

10 William Towle, the General Manager of the London Midland Co., at the Adelphi Hotel.
Bedford Lemere, 1912.

11 Bedroom 159. Bedford Lemere, 1912.

DAISH'S HOTEL, SHANKLIN, ISLE OF WIGHT, AND ESPLANADE HOTEL, VENTNOR, ISLE OF WIGHT

The popularity of the Isle of Wight was boosted by Queen Victoria's fondness for the Island and the arrival of the railway, which reached Shanklin in 1864 and Ventnor in 1866. Ferries arrived from the mainland at Ryde, Cowes, Yarmouth and Ventnor.

A greatly enlarged Daish's Hotel advertised in the U.D.C. *Official Guide*: 'an omnibus and carriages meet all trains . . . The original American Bar. Smartest Rendezvous in the Island.'

12 Daish's Hotel, Shanklin, in the 1860s. Copyright Howarth-Loomes Collection.

13 Esplanade Hotel, Ventnor, in the 1860s. Copyright Howarth-Loomes Collection.

14 EASTHAM FERRY HOTEL, EASTHAM, MERSEYSIDE

Kelly's *Directory of Cheshire 1928* says of Eastham: 'This place in the summer months is a favourite resort for pleasure and picnic parties from Liverpool by ferry across the river'. The Manchester Ship Canal enters the Mersey here. The hotel was immediately opposite the pay gates of the ferry at the shore end. The Eastham Ferry, the oldest on the river, was converted to a steam ferry in 1868 and the hotel, originally built by Sir Thomas Stanley *c* 1846, is appropriately ornamented in the 'steamboat' style. Bedford Lemere, 1897.

15 QUEEN'S HOTEL, BIRMINGHAM, WEST MIDLANDS.

Designed by William Livock and opened in 1854, the hotel forms part of the New Street Station complex. Additions were made to it in 1911 and 1917. NMR, 1966.

16 FIRST-CLASS REFRESHMENT ROOM, CENTRAL STATION, NEWCASTLE-UPON-TYNE, TYNE AND WEAR.

The railway station, John Dobson's last large scheme in Newcastle, was opened in 1850 though the building was not completed until 1865.

The photograph of the first-class refreshment room was not taken until 1893 but apparently the provinces still preferred to eat at large tables rather than in more intimate groupings.
Bedford Lemere, 1893.

17 WESTMINSTER PALACE HOTEL, VICTORIA STREET, LONDON

The first attempt to rectify the lack of good hotel accommodation in the capital, the hotel was built on the site of Caxton's house in 1860. Designed by W. and A. Moseley, it was not only the most luxurious hotel in London but was also courageously situated some distance from any of the main railway termini. Its 286 letting rooms were intended to provide accommodation for Members of Parliament and visitors to the Law Courts, then centred in Westminster. Five men were killed and eight injured when scaffolding collapsed during construction of the hotel.

The building was eventually converted into offices and renamed Abbey House before demolition in the 1970s. Newton and Co., *c* 1880.

18 GROSVENOR HOTEL, VICTORIA STATION, LONDON.

Designed by J. T. Knowles, the hotel was erected by the London, Brighton and South Coast Railway and subsequently leased by the Gordon Hotel Co. The foundations are on part of the old Grosvenor Basin.

The photograph shows the hall. Bedford Lemere, 1910.

19 ILFRACOMBE HOTEL, ILFRACOMBE, DEVON.
The railway provided a clientele for this seaside hotel, designed by C. W. Hornes and built in 1863. Foreign package holidays must have contributed to the causes of its closure and subsequent demolition in the late 1970s.

The photograph shows a lamp supporter on the newel of the staircase. NMR, 1975.

20 SALISBURY HOTEL AND FARMERS' CLUB, SALISBURY SQUARE, FLEET STREET, LONDON.
This rather 'old style' hotel was erected by the Agricultural Hotel Company in 1863–4. The architect was John Giles and the cost of building about 100 rooms was £23 000. The hotel was popular with landowners and farmers.

The group in the photograph was taken in the same year as the hotel's closure in 1910 after which time the building became the offices of *The Times of India*. Bedford Lemere, 1910.

21 STAR AND GARTER HOTEL,
RICHMOND, GREATER LONDON.
Designed in 1864 by Edward Middleton
Barry, son of Sir Charles Barry and architect
of hotels at Charing Cross and Cannon Street
Stations. After a fire in 1870 the hotel was
rebuilt to the design of C. J. Phipps. The Star
and Garter Hotel had extensive gardens and
was very popular with day trippers, often on
bicycles from London, and with evening
diners for its romantic setting overlooking
the Thames. Photographer unknown, *c* 1900.

22 GRAND HOTEL, SCARBOROUGH,
N. YORKSHIRE.
The Grand Hotel by Cuthbert Broderick,
architect of Leeds Town Hall, was built in
1867 of yellow and red brick. This was
Broderick's last great work before retiring,
aged forty-seven, to France.

   The hotel was open only in July and
August.

   The photograph must have been taken
shortly after the hotel was completed.
Copyright Howarth-Loomes Collection,
c 1870.

NORTH WESTERN HOTEL, LIME STREET,
LIVERPOOL, MERSEYSIDE.
Built in 1868–71, the North Western Hotel
was designed by Alfred Waterhouse to be
integrated with Lime Street Station. Close to
the Adelphi Hotel, it doubtless catered for
the same type of clientele – travellers to and
from America. Latterly the North Western
Hotel fared less well than its neighbour,
becoming offices named Lime Street
Chambers.

23 The west façade. NMR, 1970.

24 A detail of the old North Western Railway
coat of arms on the central east façade.
NMR, 1970.

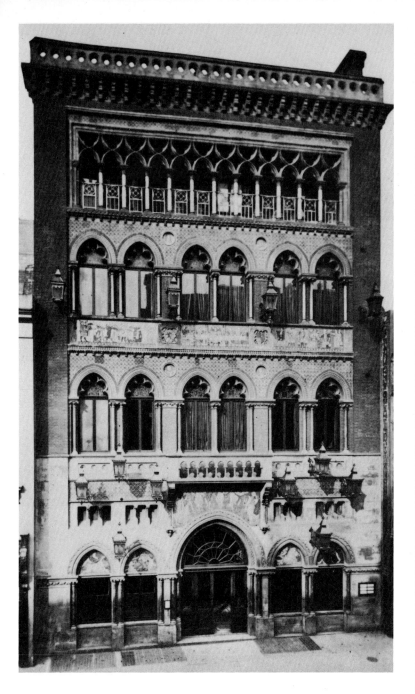

25 ST JAMES' HALL AND RESTAURANT, PICCADILLY, LONDON.
A concert hall and restaurant opened in April 1858 and extended in 1875. The
façade was designed by Owen Jones.

 The menu included Grilled Bones, Roast Quails, Pickled Salmon and
Lobster.

 The Piccadilly Hotel, designed by Norman Shaw 1905–8, now occupies the
site. Bedford Lemere, *c* 1875. Copyright Christopher Wood Gallery.

26 PIMM'S, 3 POULTRY, LONDON.
A chop-house opened in 1870, owned by the brother-in-law of Frederick
Gordon, Horatio Davies, who later became Lord Mayor of London.

 Pimm's drinks are named after the restaurant where they were served.
G. Green, 1946.

MIDLAND GRAND HOTEL, ST. PANCRAS STATION, LONDON.

The hotel was designed by Sir George Gilbert Scott in the Gothic style and opened on 5 May 1873, incomplete. The cost was £438 000, four times as much as the Westminster Palace Hotel. There was much criticism of the expensive features, considered by some to be overdone. Gillows furnished the hotel. The manager was Robert Etzensberger from the Victoria Hotel, Venice.

The hotel closed in 1935 and the building is now used as offices by British Rail. A start has been made on cleaning the façade.

27 The main staircase. NMR, 1967.

28 An alcove on the first-floor landing. NMR, 1967.

29 CRITERION RESTAURANT, PICCADILLY CIRCUS, LONDON.
Designed by Thomas Verity in 1873 for Spiers and Pond, the restaurant is on the site of the White Bear Inn and adjoins the Criterion Theatre. In 1894, according to Baedeker, a table d'hôte dinner cost 3s.6d., attendance 3d, and was served between the hours of 5.30 and 8 p.m. accompanied by 'glees and songs'. Cocktails were served in the bar.

The photographs shows the Victoria Hall with the Grand Hall beyond. Bedford Lemere, 1913.

30 HOLBORN VIADUCT HOTEL, LONDON.
Designed in 1874 by Isaacs and Florence for Spiers and Pond. The catering at the nearby Holborn Viaduct Station was by the same company.

The photograph shows the dining-room. Bedford Lemere, 1901.

HOLBORN RESTAURANT, HIGH HOLBORN, LONDON.
Originally the Holborn Casino. The whole was remodelled by Archer and Green 1884, the corner by
Colcutt 1894. The Holborn Restaurant was owned by Frederick Gordon. It could cater for the banqueting
trade with its large number of different rooms.

31 (*previous page*) The Crown Room just before the contents of the restaurant were auctioned. Herbert
Felton, 1955.

32 The Grand Salon. Bedford Lemere, 1935.

33 FIRST AVENUE HOTEL, HIGH HOLBORN, LONDON.
Opened by Gordon Hotels in 1883, it was so named because Frederick
Gordon was much taken with the American style of street numbering.
Maples had a £70 000 contract for the furnishings. The hotel became a
popular place for barristers and solicitors to take luncheon. Bedford
Lemere, 1884.

34 GRAND HOTEL, NORTHUMBERLAND AVENUE, LONDON.
Frederick Gordon's first hotel. It was designed by Messrs. Francis and
opened in 1881. The photograph shows the ornate Grand Salle.
Non-residents were welcome to dine in the hotel. Bedford Lemere, 1912.

35 METROPOLE HOTEL, NORTHUMBERLAND AVENUE, LONDON.
Opened in 1885, the architects were F. and H. Francis and J. E. Saunders. It was the second hotel in
Northumberland Avenue owned by Frederick Gordon, the first being the Grand Hotel designed by Francis
and opened in 1881. The Metropole was often used by the then Prince of Wales.
  The photograph shows a horse brake outside the hotel. The fare for a trip to Kew and Richmond in a
carriage, with one horse and a coachman, was £1. 4s. Edward J. Farmer, *c* 1905.

36 (*opposite*) MIDLAND HOTEL, BRADFORD, WEST YORKSHIRE.
Designed in 1885 by Trubshaw, Chief Architect of the Midland Railway, the hotel rivalled the Victoria
Hotel (Lockwood and Mawson) erected in 1867 close to Bradford Exchange Station, (originally Lancashire
and Yorkshire Railway, later L.N.E.R.).
  Sir Henry Irving died at the Midland Hotel in 1905. The photograph shows the liberal use of
Burmantofts Co. faience tiles made by the Leeds Fireclay Company. Through the window can be seen cabs
waiting at the railway station. Bedford Lemere, 1890.

Designed by Banister Fletcher, the restaurant was conveniently situated near Oxford Circus or Regent Circus as it was often known. The photograph was taken in the 1880s. Bedford Lemere.

39 (*opposite*) BERKELEY HOTEL, PICCADILLY, LONDON.
Opened in 1888, altered in 1897, and purchased by D'Oyly Carte in 1901. He wanted to obtain George Reeves-Smith, managing director of the Berkeley, as a replacement for Cézar Ritz at the Savoy. Ritz and Escoffier had removed to the Carlton.

The restaurant of the Berkeley was always popular and smart for lunch and dinner. Debutantes and their mothers often took tea at the hotel. In 1953 the Berkeley Debutante Dress Show was started and is still part of the London season.

The hotel closed on 3 August 1969, and a new Berkeley Hotel opened in Wilton Place in February 1972.

The photograph shows the Smoking Room by S. J. Waring. Bedford Lemere, 1897.

38 VIENNA CAFÉ, 24–28 NEW OXFORD STREET, LONDON.
The Vienna Café, opened by the Anglo-Austrian Confectionery Co. *c* 1885, was on a site at the junction of New Oxford Street and Hart Street (now Bloomsbury Way). It was a Continental-type café which encouraged patrons to spend some time on the premises by making available periodicals, chess and billiards.

The photograph of the downstairs café shows a tempting range of cakes and chocolates. Presumably more substantial meals were served in the area provided with tablecloths and cruets. The upstairs room was simpler in style. Bedford Lemere, 1897.

HYDE PARK HOTEL, KNIGHTSBRIDGE, LONDON.

Designed in 1888 by Archer and Green for Jabez Balfour as a block of flats named Hyde Park Court. The original Hyde Park Hotel was in Hyde Park Place near Marble Arch.

Following a fire, the building was converted to an hotel in 1900. Mewès and Davis assisted with the décor.

Nathaniel Newnham-Davis includes a menu from this hotel in *The Gourmet's Guide to London*, 1914:

> Caviar Blinis
> Créme d'Asperges
> Sole à la H.P.H.
> Selle d'Agneau de lait poelée
> Haricots verts aux finesherbes
> Bécassines Chausseur
> Salade
> Pêches Petit Duc
> Comtesse Marie
> Friandises
> Dessert

M. Muller, the *chef de cuisine*, invented a vegetable sorbet – *tomates givrées*.

40 The photograph shows one of two panels which were in the new Restaurant. The panels were executed by Georges Rémon and Cie and are inscribed,
'Peinture Originale par Hubert Robert. Autrefois à l'hôtel de Suynes à Paris Ensuite dans la collection du Duc de Gramont'.

They were obviously similar to panels from the same source used by Mewès and Davis for the Royal Automobile Club in Pall Mall. Bedford Lemere, c 1920s

41 and **42** Designs for panels. Copyright Mewès and Davis

46 CAFÉ MONICO, SHAFTESBURY
AVENUE, LONDON.
Designed by Christopher and White in 1888, it contained a restaurant, grill room, café and luncheon bar.
A concert hall called the International Hall was situated above the café.
  The photograph is of the buffet. Bedford Lemere, 1915.

SAVOY HOTEL, STRAND, LONDON.
The river block was designed by T. E. Collcutt and opened in 1889 by Sir Richard D'Oyly Carte. The hotel
was close to D'Oyly Carte's Savoy Theatre.
  The Strand block was built in 1903–4 also to the designs of Collcutt.
  The emphasis was on luxury. The hotel had six hydraulic lifts, seventy bathrooms and electric light
throughout. Arthur Mackmurdo was concerned with the interior furnishings and there were William
Morris wallpapers and William de Morgan pottery.
  Cézar Ritz and Escoffier were brought to the hotel in 1890. Escoffier transformed the visually arresting
but tepid food by introducing an assembly line to put dishes together. The success of this system enabled
Escoffier to provide an *à la carte* menu served to the accompaniment of waltzes played by Johan Strauss.

47 A bedroom, 1893.

48 The Salle à Manger, 1898.

49 (*overleaf*) The Lounge. Bedford Lemere, 1904.

HOTEL CECIL, STRAND, LONDON.

Designed by Archer and Green and erected 1890–96 on the west side of the Savoy. A Jabez Balfour (Liberator Building Co.) hotel for which he did not produce the necessary finance and was sentenced in 1895 to fourteen years penal servitude. The liquidator got extra money from the original shareholders to finish the hotel, which was at the time the largest in Europe. The overheads were high but the hotel had good facilities and was popular, in particular with Americans and businessmen. The décor of the Restaurant had to be changed as it was too gloomy. Later a Palm Court was built over part of the forecourt, known to American visitors as The Beach as it was supplied with a news-stand, easy chairs, drinks brought by waiters and possessed an air of gaiety.

Between 1917 and 1920 the building was requisitioned by the Air Board and the hotel finally closed on 23 February 1930. It was demolished in sixteen weeks and Shell-Mex acquired the site.

50 The Grand Hall. Bedford Lemere, 1899.

51 The Hairdressing Saloon.
Bedford Lemere, 1911.

52 (*opposite*) HANS PLACE HOTEL, EXETER STREET, LONDON.
The exterior was designed by Read and Macdonald *c* 1895. Within a year of its opening the hotel changed its name to the Hans Crescent Hotel to avoid confusion caused by the renaming of Exeter Street as Hans Crescent.

The photograph of the Winter Garden was taken in 1896. Diners had tables in the Winter Garden reserved with the same number as their table in the restaurant. After dinner, coffee and liqueurs could be taken in the Winter Garden to the sound of M. Casano's band. Bedford Lemere, 1896.

53 METROPOLE HOTEL, WEST LEAS, FOLKESTONE, KENT.
Designed by Thomas Cutler for Gordon Hotels Ltd in 1896 and decorated by Smee and Tobay.

Tourists invaded Folkestone, and the Metropole, feeling its select image threatened, tried to block public access to the Leas which fronted the hotel.

The photograph shows the spacious and ornate Billiard Room. Bedford Lemere, 1897.

54 (*overleaf*) MIDLAND HOTEL, MANCHESTER, GREATER MANCHESTER.
Designed by Charles Trubshaw in 1898, his last work. The hotel was built of brick, terracotta, and red and grey Aberdeen granite. An annexe was designed in 1930 by Sir Edwin Lutyens but was not built due to the depression.

Businessmen and travellers using the nearby Central Station were entertained with après-luncheon concerts in the Palm Court. It was in the Palm Court that Charles Rolls and Henry Royce first met in 1904. Bedford Lemere, 1912.

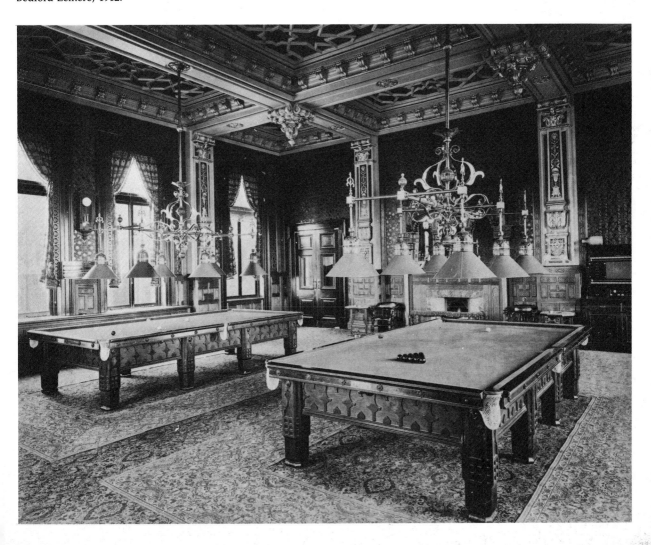

TOWER BRIDGE HOTEL, TOWER BRIDGE ROAD, LONDON.
Designed by W. A. Withall in 1897, the hotel was more in the tradition of an inn with dining-room and some accommodation. It was situated on a main thoroughfare near the docks, London Bridge Station and Bermondsey Leather Market, and catered largely for the recreational tastes of the working man.

55 The Tower Bridge Hotel. Bedford Lemere, 1897.

56 The kitchen. Bedford Lemere, 1897.

57 (*opposite, above*) The skittle alley. Bedford Lemere, 1897.

58 (*opposite, below*) The wine and spirit cellar. Bedford Lemere, 1897.

59 (*opposite*) PRINCES RESTAURANT, PICCADILLY, LONDON.

Designed by Wimperis and Arber *c* 1895, utilizing the room below the gallery of the Institute of Painters in Water Colour. The Princes Hotel was in part of the same building.

The Restaurant was a popular place for stage and society ladies to eat luncheon. Bedford Lemere, 1896.

60 (*above*) TROCADERO, SHAFTESBURY AVENUE, LONDON.

Designed by W. J. Ansell and J. Hatchard Smith, the Trocadero opened in 1897 and was enlarged in 1901 (Ansell) and 1930 (F. J. Wills).

The photograph is of the Cocktail Bar. Photographer unknown, *c* 1930s.

CARLTON HOTEL, HAYMARKET, LONDON.

Built in 1897–9 to the designs of Phipps and H. L. Florence, the Carlton was managed by Cézar Ritz. Mewès and Davis were responsible for the decor; the walls were painted because Ritz considered wallpaper unhygienic. Double windows were fitted. Escoffier came with Ritz from the Savoy and again produced an *à la carte menu*.

The Carlton was damaged by bombs during the war and was eventually demolished. The site is now occupied by New Zealand House.

61 The south entrance. Herbert Felton, 1957.

62 The staircase. Bedford Lemere, 1928.

63 GREAT CENTRAL HOTEL, MARYLEBONE, LONDON.
Opened in 1899, the architect was Colonel Edis, who designed part of the Great Eastern Hotel, Liverpool
Street Station. The building was paid for by Sir Blundell Maple and owned by the Frederick Group,
probably because the Great Central Railway Co. could not raise the necessary finance themselves. The
hotel was, of course, furnished by Maples and had the almost obligatory Winter Garden with orchestra.
Bedford Lemere, 1899.

RIDGWAY'S CAFÉ, MANCHESTER,
GREATER MANCHESTER.
Designed by T. Arnold Ashworth in Arts and
Crafts style, the café was fronted by a tea
shop selling Ridgways tea.

64 (*opposite*) The shop front. Bedford Lemere,
1901.

65 The Smoke Room. Bedford Lemere, 1901.

66 A view to the Ladies Room. Bedford
Lemere, 1901.

FELIX HOTEL, COBBOLD ROAD, FELIXSTOWE, SUFFOLK.
Designed 1900–3 by Hon. Douglas Tollemache and T. W. Cotman, and owned by the L.N.E.R., it was described by H. Clunn in *The Face of the Home Counties* (1936) as 'quite the most splendid hotel on the east coast'.

There was a Winter Garden, 28 tennis courts and a croquet lawn. Later, hot and cold sea water baths, massage baths etc. were provided.

The L.N.E.R. advertised in its Tariffs of Hotels: 'combined rail and hotel weekend tickets during certain seasons'. After the hotel had closed, it was acquired by Messrs Fisons who renamed it Harvest House.

67 The exterior, N.M.R., 1974.

68 An advertisement for the hotel. 1908.

SEPTEMBER is a charming Month to visit THE FELIX HOTEL FELIXSTOWE.

Felixstowe occupies a unique position—though situated on the East Coast, faces DUE SOUTH, thus combining the BRACING AIR of the German Ocean with an excess of BRILLIANT SUNSHINE over all South Coast Resorts. Minimum rainfall.
Celebrated for its Health-Restoring Climate.

THE MOST ATTRACTIVE HOTEL AND GROUNDS ON THE ENGLISH COAST.

UNUSUAL FACILITIES FOR OUTDOOR RECREATION.

Facing South and Sea.   Sheltered Balconies.   250 Rooms.   Charming Suites.   Garage.
Lovely Gardens and Terraced Walks to the Beach.   BLUE HUNGARIAN BAND.
MODERATE INCLUSIVE TERMS.
Telephone 99.   **Non-Stop Trains** leave Liverpool St. daily, 1.56 p.m. and 4.10 p.m.   Write for Descriptive Booklet.

GOLF, CROQUET, TENNIS, BOATING, BATHING, FISHING.

69 IMPERIAL HYDRO, BLACKPOOL, LANCASHIRE.
Designed by J. B. Broadbent, architect of the Albion Hotel, Manchester. Catering for the prevailing taste at the time, the Imperial provided many different types of bath including Turkish, Russian, Sitz, Needle Spray, rain, plunge, warm, cold and sea water.

The photograph shows the Smoking Room. Bedford Lemere, 1898.

70 POPULAR CAFÉ, PICCADILLY, LONDON.
Designed by C. W. Oakley for J. Lyons. Following the success of a subterranean restaurant in Throgmorton Street, Lyons opened the Popular Café in 1904. Bedford Lemere, 1904.

RUMPELMAYER (LATER PRUNIER), ST JAMES'S, LONDON.
A Viennese confectioner and restaurant which opened in 1906 or 1907. A member of the family had been brought by Cézar Ritz to the Carlton Hotel to advise on improvement of the coffee.

The restaurant was later altered to become Prunier. The designer was J. P. Mongeaud in collaboration with W. Henry White and Son. There were two rooms for dining. The front room had a circular lift hoist and an illuminated ceiling. The inner room had green walls and a green glass lighting panel in V-shaped troughs complemented by pink opalescent lighting from the cornice. A zig-zag glass screen at the end of the restaurant concealed the service area.

71 Rumpelmayer's. Bedford Lemere, 1910.

72 The front dining-room at Prunier, c 1935. Copyright *Architect and Building News* (B. W. S. Publishing)

RITZ HOTEL, PICCADILLY, LONDON.
Designed by Mewès and Davis 1903–6, the
Ritz, a steel-framed building, was erected on
the sites of the Walsingham House Hotel and
the Bath Hotel.

Mewès, who had designed the Paris Ritz
interiors, broke with the multi-style
decoration of the previous decade and used a
luxurious Louis XVI style throughout.

73 The Winter Garden. The chairs were
designed by Mewès and Davis and made by
Waring and Gillow. N.M.R. 1980.

74 The carpet of the vestibule near the
Arlington Street entrance. There seems to be
some doubt as to the manufacturer –
Aubusson or Savonnerie. Copyright Mewès
and Davis, *c* 1906.

75 HOTEL CURZON, CURZON STREET,
LONDON.
The hotel was situated on the corner of Clarges Street. The photograph shows a table laid for a wedding
feast. The room is decorated in the Beaux-Arts manner. Bedford Lemere, 1907.

STRAND PALACE HOTEL, STRAND, LONDON.
Designed for J. Lyons and Co., the hotel was built on the site of
Exeter Hall which was pulled down in 1907. It formed a
T-shape, as the Strand entrance was flanked on either side by
Haxell's Hotel. By 1930 Haxell's had been demolished; the
remainder of the Strand Palace Hotel was built on its site,
absorbing also the Globe newspaper building. The façade (1925–
30) was by F. J. Wills. Oliver Bernard, assisted by J. M.
Richards, created the décor, some examples of which are now
in the Victoria and Albert Museum.

76 The Winter Garden of the Strand Palace Hotel designed by
W. J. Ancell. Bedford Lemere, 1909.

77 The Strand entrance of Haxell's Hotel. Bedford Lemere, 1909.

78 The lifts of the Strand Palace Hotel. Herbert Felton, *c* 1930.

79 The Orchestra Dais, Strand Palace Hotel. Herbert Felton, *c* 1930.

80 WALDORF HOTEL, ALDWYCH, LONDON.
A steel-framed building designed by A. M. and A. G. R. Mackenzie, 1906–8. There is still a Palm Court in the hotel.

The photograph shows the Strand Theatre (formerly the Waldorf Theatre) and the Aldwych Theatre flanking the hotel. In the foreground is the site of the future India House; the new Gaiety Theatre and Restaurant just appears on the extreme left, Kingsway had recently opened in 1905 connecting the Aldwych and Holborn. Bedford Lemere, 1908.

81 IMPERIAL HOTEL, RUSSELL SQUARE, LONDON.
Designed by C. Fitzroy Doll to be erected in three parts, the first part was built in 1907 and the central block in 1911. The final section was never built.

The Turkish Bath, shown in the photograph, was situated in the central portion of the hotel. NMR, 1965.

82 (*opposite*) ROMANO'S, STRAND, LONDON
The original Romano's at No. 399 Strand was burnt down and the new restaurant, occupying an extended area, opened in 1911.

Romano's closed in 1948. Bedford Lemere, 1911.

83 (*opposite*) LYON'S CORNER HOUSE, STRAND, LONDON.
Erected in 1908. Like some other branches, e.g. in Coventry Street, this Corner House was, rather surprisingly, open all night. Bedford Lemere, 1915.

MAISON LYONS, OXFORD STREET, LONDON.
Designed by Lewis Soloman and Son, and situated on the north side of Oxford Street adjoining Lilley and Skinner, this Lyons branch opened in 1915.

84 The ground floor from the entrance. Bedford Lemere, 1916.

85 A Ragtime Band playing in the restaurant. Bedford Lemere, 1916.

86 TEA ROOMS, LIVERPOOL STREET STATION, LONDON.
The refreshment rooms here, and down the line, were in the charge of the manager of the Great Eastern
Hotel. Bedford Lemere, 1916.

87 KARSINO, TAGG'S ISLAND, HAMPTON, GREATER LONDON.
The Karsino, opened just before the First World War and owned by Fred Karno, was a complex of pleasure
resort, hotel, concert hall and boathouse. It was originally open only in the summer season. There were
café concerts daily at 3 p.m. and 8 p.m. The ferry to the island cost 6d. or a boat could be tied up for 1s.
  By 1930 the resort had changed its name to the Thames Riviera and was open all the year round.
Photographer unknown, *c* 1930s.

88 ODDENINO'S CAFÉ, 54–62 REGENT STREET,
LONDON.
Designed 1928–9 by Yates, Cook and Derbyshire, the
Café was formerly the Imperial Restaurant. It was
opened by Oddenino, an ex-Manager of the Café
Royal, who came from Turin. He had previously
opened one of the great hotels in Cimiez (Nice)
   The Café was part of Oddenino's Hotel which
opened in 1928. Herbert Felton, *c* 1929

89 DORCHESTER HOTEL, PARK LANE, LONDON.
Designed by Curtis Green in 1930 and erected on the
site of Dorchester House, the hotel was built at a cost
of £1 750 000 for Gordon Hotels. It was sold in 1936 to
McAlpines.
   The floors were lined with seaweed and the
bedrooms with cork for soundproofing. Oliver Messel
redecorated the hotel, as did Oliver Ford later. Herbert
Felton, *c* 1931.

90 HONEYDEW RESTAURANT, 39 COVENTRY STREET, LONDON.
Opened in 1932. A first Honeydew restaurant had opened at No. 356 Strand a year or two earlier. The
Coventry Street branch was a self-service café serving a drink named after the restaurant, and Ritz Carlton
Red Hots . . . Herbert Felton, *c* 1932.

FISCHER'S RESTAURANT, NEW BOND STREET, LONDON.

The architect was Raymond McGrath (1932) who also designed the furniture. The general lighting of the basement restaurant was by 'sunlight' nitrogen tubes which gave a gold-peach light. Coral-red colour was chosen for the columns as the nitrogen tubes gave a particular brilliance to this shade. The ceiling was pale yellow and the walls a straw colour. The specially designed upholstery was of green-stripe grey fabric. The dance floor was of Austrian oak strip inlaid with hornbeam and walnut. A special feature of the restaurant was the luminous tube serpent which twined across the ceiling. McGrath had revived the dying technique of brilliant cutting glass for the re-vamped Embassy Club and mirrors were treated with this method at Fischers.

The Cocktail Bar on the ground floor had a counter with a front of illuminated 'ferro-glass' and a top of polished travertine. The walls were covered with green metallic paper.

91 (*previous page*) The restaurant. Herbert Felton, c 1932. Copyright Architectural Press.

92 The staircase. Herbert Felton, *c* 1932. Copyright Architectural Press.

93 STANDARD RESTAURANT, HAYMARKET, LONDON.
The Standard Restaurant opened in 1936 situated beside the Haymarket exit of the re-vamped Piccadilly
Underground Station. There were several rooms including the Continental Bar on the ground floor and the
Haymarket Bar in the basement. The Brasserie shown in the photograph had a dance floor. Herbert Felton,
1936.

PALACE COURT HOTEL, WESTOVER ROAD, BOURNEMOUTH, DORSET.
The hotel, which included service flats, was designed in 1935 by A. J. Seal and Partners.

Bournemouth had developed late as a resort, mostly after the railway had reached it in 1870. It maintained a somewhat genteel image which attracted retired people, often from the North.

94 The exterior of the Palace Court Hotel. Herbert Felton, 1935. Copyright *The Architect and Building News* (B.W.S. Publishing).

95 The coffee lounge. Herbert Felton, 1935. Copyright *The Architect and Building News* (B.W.S. Publishing).

96 QUALITY INN, 22 LEICESTER SQUARE, LONDON.
Designed by Riley and Glanfield in 1938, its purpose was 'to provide quick well-cooked meals at reasonable cost'.
   The photograph shows the cash desk and manager's office. Herbert Felton, *c* 1938.

97 (*overleaf*) HILTON HOTEL, 21–24 PARK LANE, LONDON.
Designed 1961–3 by Lewis Soloman, Kaye and Partners, the hotel was one of the world-wide Hilton chain. It attracted much criticism for its height (405 feet). It was one of several new hotels built at the south end of Park Lane during the 1960s.
   The photograph shows the Hilton Hotel, and the Londonderry House Hotel under construction. NMR, 1966.